AR PTS: 1.0

D0852178

A History of

Railroads

by Colin Hynson

GARETH**STEVENS**

GS

P U B L I S H I N G

A Member of the WRC Media Family of Companies

Please visit our web site at: www.garethstevens.com
For a free color catalog describing Gareth Stevens Publishing's list of high-quality
books and multimedia programs, call 1-800-542-2595 (USA) or 1-800-387-3178 (Canada).
Gareth Stevens Publishing's fax: (414) 332-3567.

Library of Congress Cataloging-in-Publication Data

Hynson, Colin.
    A history of railroads / Colin Hynson.—North American ed.
        p. cm. — (From past to present)
    Includes index.
    ISBN 0-8368-6287-2 (lib. bdg.)
    1. Railroads—History—Juvenile literature. I. Title. II. Series.
  HE1021.H96   2006
  385.09—dc22   2005054076

This North American edition first published in 2006 by
Gareth Stevens Publishing
A Member of the WRC Media Family of Companies
330 West Olive Street, Suite 100
Milwaukee, WI 53212 USA

This edition copyright © 2006 by Gareth Stevens, Inc. Original edition copyright © 2003 by ticktock Entertainment Ltd.
First published in Great Britain in 2003 by ticktock Media Ltd., Unit 2, Orchard Business Center, North Farm Road,
Tunbridge Wells, Kent TN2 3XF in association with the National Maritme Museum, Greenwich. Additional end matter
copyright 2006 by Gareth Stevens, Inc.

Gareth Stevens editor: Leifa Butrick
Gareth Stevens designer: Kami M. Strunsee

The publishers would like to thank Graham Rich, John Guy, and Peter Done for their assistance.

Picture Credits: t=top, b=bottom, c=center, l=left, r=right
Ann Ronan @ Image Select; 5b, 4c, 4br, 5c, 5t, 7tl, 6b, 6br, 6c, 7cl, 9t, 9c, 8b, 8cl, 9b, 11cr, 10t, 11b, 13cl, 12b, 13br, 15cl, 14c,
15cr, 15b, 15tr, 16b, 16c, 18b, 18c, 20b, 22t, 22b, 22c, 24b, 27t, 30bl, 31b. Chris Fairclough Colour Library/Image Select; 8cr,
23c, 25cl, 27c, 30br. Colin Garratt/Milepost92´/CORBIS; 7b. CORBIS/Bettmann; 10b, 14b, 17cl, 17t, 28c. et archive; 24t, 28b.
Forabolafoto (Milan); 33b. Hulton Getty; 17cr. Image Select; 4bl, 11cl, 10cl, 13tl, 19cl, 23t, 30c, 31t. Mary Evans; 12t, 12c, 13tr,
15t, 16t, 20c, 20t, 33tl. Michael Yamashita/CORBIS; 33c. Milepost 92½; 13bl, 19cr, 21b, 25cr, 32b. Pix; 17br, 17bl, 19t, 19b, 26b,
26t, 31cr, 33tr. Science and Society Picture Library; 7tr, 11t, 18t, 25t, 29c, 32c. Spectrum Colour Library; 7cr, 26/27, 28t, 29t,
29b, 31cl. ticktock Entertainment Ltd.; 14t, 21c, 21t, 25b, 32t. Trip/C Rennie; 23b.

Printed in the United States of America

1 2 3 4 5 6 7 8 9 10 09 08 07 06

CONTENTS

Words that appear in the glossary are printed in
boldface type the first time they occur in the text.

Vehicles that traveled by rail existed long before the invention of the **steam engine**. In the ruins of Pompeii, grooves cut into the paved roads show that primitive horse-drawn railroads existed during the time of the Romans. Since the sixteenth century, wagons have run along wooden rails in mines throughout Europe. Rails improved a trip because the vehicle's wheels rolled along a smoother, straighter surface than most roads offered. Travel was still slow, however, while it relied on the muscle power of humans or animals. Although the ancient Greeks understood steam power, no one built an effective steam engine until the middle of the eighteenth century. At first, steam mostly was used as power for stationary machines. Eventually, engineers put steam to work on the railroads. Fast, long-distance travel then became a reality.

Cugnot's Steam Car

In 1769, Nicholas Cugnot, a French military engineer, produced the first moving vehicle to use steam power. His three-wheeled car moved cannons for the French army. The weight of the huge copper **boiler** at the front made the steam car difficult to steer, and on its first trip, it ran into a stone wall. The next year, Cugnot built another machine, which he demonstrated in Paris. It overturned as it tried to go around a corner. Cugnot was arrested as a public nuisance, and his machine was impounded.

Trevithick's Experiments

Richard Trevithick (1771–1833) was the first person to put vehicles with steam engines onto rails. He learned his trade working for the owners of tin mines in Cornwall, England. Deep mines filled up with water, which prevented miners from working. Trevithick developed a steam engine to pump water from the mines. He built his first steam-powered **locomotive** in 1801 and demonstrated it on Christmas Eve, pulling a car full of people up a steep hill. In 1804, he built a railroad locomotive for an ironworks in Shropshire. In 1808, he decided to show one of his trains in London. He built a circular track in one of the most fashionable parts of the city and charged people to travel in a carriage pulled by the train. The steam locomotive did not catch on with the public, and Trevithick failed to raise interest in this new form of transportation. He returned to Cornwall and continued working on stationary steam engines, including a steam threshing machine and the first rock-boring machine.

Catch Me Who Can

One reason Trevithick's trains were an improvement over earlier steam-driven vehicles was that he found a way to put the steam under high pressure. The steam engine could then be more powerful without making it bigger. Trevithick used a high-pressure steam engine on the train he showed in London. The train was called Catch Me Who Can because it traveled on a circular track.

Hauling Coal

This steam locomotive (*below*) was built by John Blenkinsop (1783–1831) in 1812. It carried coal from a coal mine to the city of Leeds, a distance of 3.5 miles (5.6 kilometers). It stayed on the tracks by means of grooves in the wheels and the tracks.

WILLS'S CIGARETTES.

HEDLEY'S PUFFING BILLY, 1813.

Puffing Billy

Many early locomotives stayed on the tracks by having grooved driving wheels and grooved rails. British engineer William Hedley (1779–1843) designed smooth train wheels with enough grip to stay on smooth tracks. In 1813, he built a train called Puffing Billy (*left*) using this new design. Puffing Billy carried coal from a mine in northern England to a nearby river.

Early attempts at steam-powered locomotion showed that long-distance travel at previously unimagined speeds was possible. British engineers George and Robert Stephenson (1781–1848 and 1803–1859), who were father and son, built reliable steam engines for customers all over the world. Within a few decades, railroad lines linked entire continents. Journeys that once took several days through dangerous country now took only a few hours, and passengers rode in safety and comfort. The steam engine provided the most common form of mass transportation until the 1950s when **diesel fuel** and electricity began driving the trains. The passion for steam engines, however, continues to this day. Many are still carefully maintained and run by railroad preservation societies. There are also some parts of the world where steam trains are still used commercially.

The Locomotion

George Stephenson convinced the owners of the Stockton and Darlington Railroad in England to use steam engines instead of horse-drawn wagons. The first locomotive he built for the railroad was the Locomotion, (*left*). It pulled twenty-eight coal-filled wagons. For the first time, a connecting rod was used between the front and back wheels, which enabled the wheels to turn together. George Stephenson built three more locomotives for the Stockton and Darlington Railroad.

Sooty Experiment

The Stockton and Darlington Railroad was the first to use steam locomotives. This engraving (*right*) shows the opening of the railroad on September 27, 1825. With 25 miles (40 km) of line, it was the longest railroad in the world. Built in an area surrounded by coal mines, it was soon carrying more than half a million tons of coal a year. The line also carried passengers. Its first passenger train, called the Experiment, was a great success.

The idea that steam could be used as a source of power existed long before the invention of the locomotive. In ancient Greece, Hero of Alexandria designed a machine that relied on steam power. It is generally accepted, however, that effective steam technology began in England, in 1698, when Thomas Savery (1650–1715) invented the Miner's Friend, a steam engine for pumping water out of mines. Thomas Newcomen (1663–1729), James Watt (1736–1819), and Matthew Boulton (1728-1809) improved Savery's invention in the eighteenth century, and by the end of that century, steam engines were at work in factories and mills, both in Europe and the United States. Richard Trevithick applied the technology to trains. Steam engines work by heating water to produce steam. The steam expands, and the resulting pressure pushes a **piston** backward and forward. The moving piston turns the wheels of the train by means of a rod and **crank**. Although the design of the steam locomotive gradually improved, the way it works has not changed significantly.

Steam from a Spout

Boiling water in a coffee pot or tea kettle illustrates the principles of steam power. The steam created by boiling water expands inside the kettle. As more is produced, it is forced out, under pressure, through the spout.

Newcomen's Steam Engine

This diagram shows a mine pump invented by Englishman Thomas Newcomen in 1712. It worked by pushing steam into a **cylinder**. As the steam cooled, it shrank, creating a vacuum. This pulled down a piston, which raised the pump rods and removed the water. The piston was then raised by weights attached to the pump rods.

Early Ideas

The illustration (*right*) comes from a book printed in 1747 called *Mathematical Elements of Natural Philosophy Confirmed by Experiments*. It shows that people were thinking about using steam power for travel more than twenty years before Cugnot built his steam car. The idea behind this vehicle was to heat water in a boiler to produce a jet of steam that would push the vehicle forward. This outcome, however, was unlikely. The vehicle would have needed a lot of fuel to produce enough steam to move it, and so much fuel would have made the vehicle too heavy. Eventually, inventors learned to put steam under pressure.

The Rainhill Contest

In October 1829, the owners of the Liverpool and Manchester Railroad announced a competition to find the best locomotive for their railroad. The five competing trains were either horse-drawn or steam-driven. The winner was the Rocket (*right*), largely designed by Robert Stephenson (*left*). It traveled 70 miles (113 km) at an average speed of 15 miles (24 km) per hour. Stephenson's victory signified the triumph of the steam engine over horse power.

The Best Friend of Charlestown

The first commercial steam engine in the United States was called the Best Friend of Charlestown. It first pulled a passenger train more than 6 miles (9.6 km) on metal and wooden rails on Christmas Day, 1830. After running successfully for several months, the locomotive exploded. The engine's **fireman** had closed the safety valve of the boiler because the noise of the engine annoyed him.

Fast and Efficient

The Flying Scotsman is one of the most famous steam engines ever made. Built in 1923, it traveled nonstop between London and Edinburgh, a distance of about 390 miles (627.5 km). At the time, that was the world's longest nonstop run. It even managed to change crews without stopping. It may have been the first train to reach 100 miles (160 km) per hour, although this cannot be verified.

Still Using Steam

Steam trains remain simple to operate and inexpensive to maintain. They still are used commercially in several countries, particularly India and China. The cost of replacing them with new diesel or electric trains can be very high. India still has nearly 5,000 steam engines in operation, and China has about 7,000. Zimbabwe repaired several of its old steam engines in the late 1970s because of the high cost of oil and the lower cost of coal.

Heating the Water

In this diagram of a steam locomotive, many tubes run the length of the locomotive. They are surrounded by water. The hot gases from the **firebox** pass through the tubes. The heat transfers to the water and produces steam.

Moving the Steam

The steam collects in a dome, called a regulator valve, then passes along a tube to a piston.

Turning the Wheels

The piston is inside a cylinder. As steam enters the cylinder, it pushes the piston forward, which then turns the wheel. Each time the piston moves forward and backward, the wheel turns through one revolution. When the piston moves backward, steam escapes. Then more steam enters the cylinder and starts the process again.

In the Cab

Two crew members always rode in the **cab** of a locomotive. The **engineer** was responsible for driving the train and regulating its speed. The fireman had to **stoke** the fire with the right amount of fuel and make sure there was water in the boiler. If there was too much steam, safety valves would shut down the engine to keep the boiler from exploding. If there was not enough steam, the train would stop.

Counting the Wheels

Locomotives are classified by the way their wheels are arranged. The small wheels at the front are called the **leading wheels**, the larger wheels connected to the pistons are the **driving wheels**, and the back wheels are known as the **trailing wheels**. Many U.S. locomotives have four leading wheels and four driving wheels but no trailing wheels. They are known as 4-4-0 type locomotives.

As railroads spread across Europe, they provided new links between cities and industrial centers. In the United States, the story was different. U.S. railroads played an important part in opening up and developing many parts of the country. Rails were laid through areas that had not yet been settled. Towns were created along the railroads to serve the needs of the railroad companies and their customers. U.S. railroads expanded into a massive system. In 1870, there were 53,000 miles (85,295 km) of track in the United States. By 1900, this figure had jumped to 190,000 miles (306,000 km), reaching a peak in 1916 of 254,000 miles (409,000 km) of U.S. track.

The Stourbridge Lion

In the early years of the steam locomotive, U.S. railroads were dominated by British engineers and factories. Between 1829 and 1841, more than one hundred locomotives were imported from England to the United States. One of the first of these locomotives was the Stourbridge Lion, which began work for the Delaware and Hudson Railroad in 1829. This locomotive proved too heavy to run effectively.

WILLS'S CIGARETTES.

1ST LOCOMOTIVE IN THE U.S.A.

Tom Thumb

In 1830, a steam locomotive called Tom Thumb and a horse-drawn train took part in a race on a stretch of the Baltimore & Ohio line. Tom Thumb broke down, and the horse won the race.

The De Witt Clinton

The first locomotive in New York State ran on August 9, 1831. As this picture (*below*) illustrates, passengers traveled on the inside and outside of the carriages. This locomotive was called the De Witt Clinton. It was named after the politician who died in 1828 after being a senator, the mayor, and the governor of New York.

U.S. Locomotives

This train (*right*) shows many of the modifications added to U.S. steam locomotives. The bars at the front, called **cowcatchers,** protected the train from being derailed by large animals such as buffaloes. Since much of the track was unprotected, a large lamp, or headlight, was placed at the front of the train to warn people of its approach. Early U.S. locomotives used wood, rather than coal, as fuel for the fireboxes, so wire mesh was placed in the smokestack to catch any sparks of burning wood.

The Last Link

In January 1863, more that 10,000 workers for the Central Pacific Railroad started to lay track eastward from Sacramento, California. In December 1865, 12,000 workers from the Union Pacific Railroad began to build new tracks westward from Omaha, Nebraska. More than three years later, the two lines met at Promontory Point, Utah. On May 10, 1869, the last spike, which was made of gold, united the two tracks. Then it was possible to take a train from the Atlantic to the Pacific coast of the United States.

Conflict with the Native Peoples

Many people who worked on the U.S. railroad system thought they were building on uninhabited land. In fact, they often were laying tracks through territory that belonged to local Native Americans. It is not surprising that the Native people attacked the trains. They saw the arrival of the railroads, and the settlements that were built around them, as a threat to their way of life.

The Railroad Craze

Railroads were successful in the United States because the public considered them a fast, inexpensive, and reliable way to travel. In the early years, U.S. railroad companies made more money from passengers than from freight.

11

After Robert Stephenson's locomotive, the Rocket, won the Rainhill contest in 1829, news of this exciting new form of transportation began to spread around the world. People from many countries went to Britain to try it out. When they returned home, they were determined to set up their own railroad systems; but for many years, Britain dominated the railroad industry. Many countries, including the United States, began their railroads by buying British-built trains. British engineers traveled around the world to supervise the laying of railroad tracks. After a while, many countries began to build their own locomotives or to modify the trains they bought so they worked better in local conditions. By the middle of the nineteenth century, the United States and Germany emerged as Britain's major competitors in building locomotives for the world market.

The Crampton

The type of train in this picture (*right*) was known as the Crampton. This British train was very popular in Europe, particularly in France. The first public railroad line in France opened in 1837 and ran between Paris and St. Germain. In the 1850s, the French railroads adopted the Crampton engine. The engines were so successful that many people referred to rail journeys as "taking the Crampton."

German Trains

At the beginning of the nineteenth century, Germany was a collection of small states. This picture (*right*) shows the first train to run in the

state of Saxony. The first train in any of the German states was the British-built Der Adler, which ran between Nuremberg and Fürth in 1835.

INDIAN STATE RLY.

An Imperial Railroad

The British controlled India in the nineteenth century, so British companies supplied most of the railroad equipment in that country. The first Indian railroad line from Bombay to Thana opened on April 18, 1853, and ran a distance of 25 miles (40 km).

Steam Engines in Japan

The first train in Japan ran on June 12, 1872, from Yokohama to Singawa. The line was extended to Tokyo by October 1872. From 1880 to 1890, the Japanese railroads grew from 98 miles (157 km) to 1,459 miles (2,350 km). In 1992 there were more than 14,500 miles (23,335km) of track in Japan.

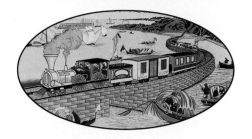

Chinese Railroads

This picture (*right*) shows the first railroad in China. It opened in 1876 and ran between Shanghai and Wuzong, a distance of 20 miles (32 km). It was only after the Chinese revolution in 1949 that railroads in China began to expand rapidly.

Swiss Mountains

Ordinary locomotives could not cope with the steep slopes of the Swiss mountains. In 1882, a Swiss engineer invented the Rack Loco (*left*). It had a toothed wheel that fit into a grooved central rail.

Dividing Africa

In the mid-1880s, the major European powers met in Berlin to divide Africa among themselves. Each resulting area developed its own railroad system, often with its own track **gauge**. When the African states gained independence, twelve different gauges of tracks were in use. This train (*left*) is a locomotive used by Nigerian Railroads.

Traveling the Continent

After India became independent in 1947, the government took over the railroad companies and modified the trains to suit local conditions. Like early trains in the United States, the Indian train in this picture (*right*) has a cowcatcher.

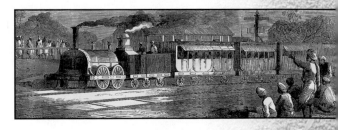

13

Building a railroad is not as simple as linking the shortest distance between two points. As Swiss railroad builders discovered, trains could not climb steep mountains. Builders had the choice of laying track around the mountains, which saved money but lost time, or of carving passages through the mountains, which saved time but cost more money. The first railroad tunnel was built in 1826 on the Manchester to Liverpool line and was about 1 mile (1.6 km) long. The longest railroad tunnel in the world is the Seikan tunnel in Japan, which is about 33 miles (53 km) long. To cross rivers and valleys, railroads needed bridges. The first railroad bridge was built on the Stockton to Darlington line in England in 1824. The longest railroad bridge in the world today is the Huey P. Long Bridge in New Orleans, which is more than 4.3 miles (7 km) long. Thousands of laborers contributed to these lasting monuments to modern engineering, and some of them lost their lives in the process.

Isambard Kingdom Brunel

One of the greatest railroad engineers of the nineteenth century was Isambard Kingdom Brunel (1806–1859). He started work with his father, building the first successful tunnel under the Thames River in London. In 1833, Brunel became an engineer for the Great Western Railroad and supervised laying the line between London and Bristol.

Foreign Laborers

Railroad building required many workers, and railroad companies relied on foreign laborers. About 10,000 Chinese laborers went to California during the 1850s and built the railroad over the Sierras and Rockies. The people who laid the tracks were called **gandy dancers**. They were named after a type of shovel they used.

Paying for the Railroad

Governments often financed railroad building because they realized railroads were important to the economies of their countries. To raise money, governments issued shares. When people bought shares, they became part owners of the railroad companies and shared the profits. Governments also made sure that sufficient land was available for the railroads. Today, governments own or support railroad lines in many countries.

Tools of the Trade

This picture (*right*) from *Punch* magazine is called *Navvy in Heavy Marching Order*. It shows many of the tools used by the laborers who built the railroads. Alongside the pick and shovel is a **coal scuttle** for carrying bricks and a small wheelbarrow to carry away rocks. The word ***navvy*** came from "navigators." Laborers employed to dig canals were called internal navigators, and many of them worked on the railroads as well.

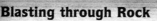

Blasting through Rock

During the early years of railroad building, laborers had to cut through solid rock using only picks and shovels. Alfred Nobel (1833–1896) made this part of railroad building much less backbreaking. In 1867, Nobel made the highly explosive liquid **nitroglycerin** safe to use by mixing it with a porous solid. He called his new invention dynamite.

Crossing Rivers

Because railroads pass through all kinds of territory, it became necessary to build all kinds of bridges. A normal arched bridge is not adequate for a train crossing a wide river or valley. The Forth Railroad Bridge, which opened in 1810 to link Edinburgh and Dundee in Scotland, (*right*) was one of the first cantilever bridges. Cantilever bridges are made of tubular steel towers joined together by a series of cables and brackets.

Railroad Stations and Signal Towers

As passengers began to use trains more and more, it became clear that they needed platforms and shelters while they waited for the trains. In 1835, in the German town of Nuremberg, a wooden shelter over a raised wooden platform became the world's first railroad station. As the nineteenth century progressed, railroad stations became larger and more ornate. Railroad companies employed the best architects and engineers to design their stations, which were sometimes called temples of steam. As the number of lines and the number of stations grew, it became increasingly important to control trains. Collisions between trains happened often in the early days of steam. Railroad companies used several methods to ensure that passengers traveled not only comfortably, but also safely.

Signal Blades

One of the earliest methods of communicating with engineers of moving trains was by using **signal blades**. The upper blades told the engineer whether the train should stop or go. The lower blades were an advance warning for the next set of signals. The signal in this picture (*right*) is telling the engineer to proceed with caution.

Early Signal Tower

Railroad lines were split up into "blocks," and a **signal tower** (*left*) controlled each block. The levers inside the signal tower controlled both signal blades and **junctions** by means of cables (shown at the *bottom* of the picture) that led from the signal tower to the various signals and junctions within each block.

Keeping in Touch

It was important for signal towers to warn each other of problems in their blocks. In 1839, the railroads first used the telegraph, invented in 1837 by William Cooke (1806–1879) and Charles Wheatstone (1802–1875), to communicate between Paddington in London with West Drayton, a distance of about 13 miles (21 km).

WILLS'S CIGARETTES.

FIVE-NEEDLE TELEGRAPH INSTRUMENT.

Modern Signal Tower

Computerized systems now operate railroad signals. The computer screens show the positions of the junctions where trains can change tracks. They also show all the signals and the locations of any trains in the area. The signals and junctions are controlled electronically.

Ticketing

The first train tickets were issued in the 1840s. They were copper discs with the passengers' destinations engraved on them. Later, paper tickets with more detail were used. Tickets were checked by guards at first; then later, by machines.

Grand Central Station

Whitney Warren designed New York City's Grand Central Station. It was under construction from 1907 to 1913 and cost $43 million to build, which was a lot of money at the time for a public building. It could not be called a temple of steam because it was built to be used only by electric locomotives.

New Stations

Even though railroads have declined in importance since the invention of automobiles and airplanes, projects to build grand railroad stations continue today. This picture (*right*) shows D'Herouville station in Lyon, France. Building new stations encourages people to use the railroads again and helps redevelop run-down urban areas. A fine railroad station still symbolizes the importance of a city.

Well before the invention of steam locomotives, horse-drawn trains pulled cars or wagons that carried goods. These trains usually were used near coal mines and traveled only short distances to nearby rivers or canals. When steam locomotives appeared, trains suddenly could pull much more than two or three cars. As railroad lines spread, two more things happened. First, goods could be taken greater distances by train, which cut out the need for trips by water. Second, trains began to carry finished goods, as well as raw materials such as coal, from factories to towns. Although **freight trains** are no longer the main way to transport goods in the United States and Europe, many Asian countries still depend on them. One type of freight that trains carried very successfully was mail. The first special postal train ran between London and Bristol, England, in February 1855. Before this time, mail coaches carried letters along muddy roads and were slow and unreliable.

Picking Up the Mail

Trains were able to pick up letters without stopping. Letters were put into a bag that hung from a special hook, as shown in this picture (*left*). As a train sped past, a net suspended from the side of the train caught the mail bag.

Sorting the Mail

Collected mail went to a special railroad car where it was sorted into pigeonholes. The sorted letters were then dropped off at designated stations. The train did not have to stop to drop off mail. The mailbag was hung over the side of the train and was caught by a net on the railroad platform. The bag was then taken away for delivery.

Early Freight Trains

Early freight steam trains used the same cars as horse-drawn trains. These trains moved slowly because none of the cars had brakes. When the problem of brakes was solved in the 1870s, trains could travel much faster.

Following Imperial Routes

The first railroad lines built in Asia served the interests of Europeans who controlled these areas, rather than the interests of native inhabitants. Passenger trains, therefore, were less important than freight trains. As this picture (*right*) shows, countries such as India still rely on the trains and the track built in the early part of the twentieth century.

Freight Trains Today

In many parts of the world, the steam engine is still the main source of power for freight trains and the dominant way of moving goods around. This is especially true in large countries such as China, where this picture (*left*) was taken. Behind the locomotive are freight cars called **flatcars**. They are the simplest kind of railroad car. Other types of freight cars are **tank cars**, which carry liquids, and **boxcars**, which enclose the freight.

Hauling Goods

This train (*right*) is operated by a U.S. railroad company and is able to pull many boxcars. By the 1930s, diesel and diesel-electric locomotives had become more powerful than steam locomotives and could pull much more freight. Many governments are concerned about the amount of freight being hauled on the roads because it causes congestion and pollution. They are trying to encourage companies to use railroads to move their goods.

The idea of electricity as a source of power was understood many years before anyone found a practical use for it. In 1800, Italian Alessandro Volta invented the battery, which gave a constant supply of electricity, and in 1819, Danish scientist Hans Christian Oersted discovered the relationship between electricity and magnetism. Two years later, English scientist Michael Faraday built the first electric motor. Electric motors work with magnets. Unlike steam engines that make their own power inside the locomotive, electric trains run on an outside source of power. Thomas Davenport demonstrated the first electric train in the United States in 1835. In 1842, an electric train ran between Edinburgh and Glasgow in Scotland. Its top speed was 4 miles (6.4 km) per hour. It was another thirty-seven years before the first serviceable electric train was built.

Werner von Siemens

The inventor of the first practical electric train came from a family of engineers and inventors. He first showed his electric train at the Berlin Trades Exhibition in 1879. The train ran on an oval track about 300 yards (275 meters) long at a speed of 4 miles (6.4 km) per hour. In 1881, the first public electric train ran near Berlin.

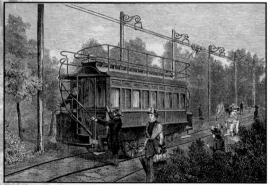

Receiving Power

This picture (*left*) of a Siemens electric train at the Paris exhibition of 1881 shows how some electric trains received their power. A **pantograph** on top of the train collected electricity from overhead cables. Other electric trains received their power from a third "live" track, laid next to the tracks that the train ran on.

Electric Trolley Car

This rather extraordinary **trolley** (*right*) ran for 3 miles (4.8 km) on rails on the beach between Brighton and Rottingdean in the early 1900s. It was built by Magnus Volk (1851–1937). Volk was also responsible for the first electric train to run in England. The train first ran on August 4, 1883, in the seaside town of Brighton.

Electric Trains in the United States

In June of 1895, a passenger service near New York used the first electric trains to operate in the United States. They ran for a distance of 7 miles (11 km). The train shown here (*right*) is the first U.S. freight train to use electricity. It first ran on August 4, 1895, on the Baltimore & Ohio Railroad, for a distance of nearly 4 miles (6.4 km). Almost half this journey was through tunnels, which was the reason for using electricity rather than steam.

The TGV

One of the fastest trains in the world is an electric train. The Train à Grande Vitesse, or TGV (*left*), first ran between Paris and Lyon, France, in September 1981. By 1988, the TGV was reaching speeds of more than 200 miles (320 km) per hour.

In the City

Streetcars have run on city streets for many years. At first, horses pulled them. Steam locomotives were not welcome on the streets of many cities because of the noise and pollution they created. The invention of the electric train meant that more streetcars could be developed in cities. For safety reasons, streetcars, like this Japanese model, usually get their power through a pantograph and overhead cables. Streetcars are an important form of public transportation in the world's cities.

Another major source of power for trains is the diesel engine. A diesel engine is a type of internal combustion engine that is similar to a gasoline engine. In 1912, the North British Locomotive Company was the first to use diesel trains, but on an experimental basis. Diesel was first used regularly in 1913 in Sweden. U.S. trains used diesel engines after 1923, and British trains used them after 1931. Electric and diesel trains now dominate railroads all over the world. Diesel engines are used either to run the engine of the train or, more commonly, to run a generator that produces an electric current to drive an electric motor. Trains that use diesel power with an electric motor are called diesel-electric locomotives.

Rudolph Diesel

There is some dispute about who invented the diesel engine. Some people claim that Herbert Akroyd-Stuart (1864–1927) built the first one in 1890. Most people, however, agree that Dr. Rudolph Diesel (1858–1913), a French-born German engineer, invented the diesel engine. Between 1880 and 1890, he searched for an efficient replacement for the steam engine. He first demonstrated the diesel engine in 1893, but he did not build the first reliable engine until 1897. In 1913, he disappeared overboard while crossing the English Channel.

How a Diesel Engine Works

Diesel engines work using a system known as **fuel injection**. Heavy diesel fuel is injected into a cylinder. A piston compresses the air inside the cylinder. Compression makes the air extremely hot, causing the fuel inside the piston to ignite and explode. The explosion pushes the piston forward. On diesel trains, the piston is then driven back by the revolving rod and crank attached to the wheels, which compresses the air inside the cylinder, which starts the whole cycle again. To control the power of the engine, the engineer varies the amount of fuel that enters the cylinder. In diesel-electric trains, the piston supplies power to a **dynamo** that produces the electrical power needed to turn the wheels.

The Deltic

One of the most successful diesel-electric engines built in Britain was the Deltic. The British began to look for a replacement for their long-distance steam trains after World War II. This prototype for the Deltic (*left*) was built in the late 1940s. It was put into production in 1955, and twenty-two Deltic engines were built in the next six years. They replaced steam trains that ran between London and Edinburgh. These trains could reach speeds of 160 miles (257 km) per hour or more, and each one has traveled more than 2 million miles (3.2 million km).

High-Speed Travel

In 1957, the members of the European Community created an international network of fast and reliable trains. The TEE (Trans Europe Express) was an attempt to compete with airline companies and was aimed at business people. It has only first-class seats. Diesel engines run all TEE trains.

Lack of Electricity

In many countries, replacing steam trains with electric trains is not practical. Many lines are not used very often, and it would be too expensive to buy electric trains and the overhead cables that are needed to run them. Diesel is the preferred replacement.

The Dominance of Diesel

Worldwide, diesel is the most popular replacement for steam because diesel trains are relatively inexpensive to buy and run. The U.S. railroad company Amtrak has nearly 24,500 miles (40,000 km) of track, but only 344 miles (553 km) are electrified. In 1994, 318 trains ran on Amtrak tracks. Sixty-five ran with electricity, and 253 used diesel engines.

Building railroad systems throughout the world made many remote and inaccessible places easier to reach. Developments in railroad engineering meant there were no conditions that could not eventually be overcome. Once impassable deserts, forests, and mountains were no longer obstacles to travel. Not only was it possible to travel to new places, but the train journeys themselves were spectacular, passing through some of the most awe-inspiring scenery in the world.

Background for Intrigue

For many, a trip on the Orient Express was the most glamorous of all train journeys. This train has been the scene for many thrillers, such as Agatha Christie's *Murder on the Orient Express*. Real-life, onboard romances, such as millionaire Sir Basil Zaharoff falling in love with a Spanish duchess while traveling to Istanbul, have added to the image.

Across the Rockies

The first train to travel the length of Canada set off from Montreal on June 28, 1886, and arrived at Port Moody one week later. The tracks later extended to Vancouver. Another transcontinental line was added in 1915, north of the first line. The Quebec Bridge, which is more than 3,000 feet (914 m) long, is on this second line.

A Train through Africa

The first luxury trains in Africa ran between Pretoria and Cape Town in 1939. Today, the Blue Train runs between Cape Town in South Africa and Victoria Falls on the Zimbabwe/Zambia border. The end of **apartheid** made it possible for train travel to continue into the heart of Africa. The Blue Train passes Table Mountain, the diamond-mining center of Kimberley, the Hwange Game Reserve, the Zambezi River, and Victoria Falls. It is one of the most beautiful journeys in the world.

Across Frozen Wastes

The Trans-Siberian Railroad runs from Moscow in the west to Vladivostock in the east. The track is nearly 6,000 miles (9,654 km) long, and traveling its entire length takes an average of eight days.

The Bullet Train

The Shinkansen runs past Mount Fuji, a dormant volcano. This line opened in 1964, and its trains travel between Tokyo and Osaka at 160 miles (257 km) per hour.

Although electric and diesel trains have replaced steam locomotives all over the world, many people still regard steam engines with affection. Steam engines seem to symbolize the power of the railroad engine much more graphically than any modern train. Steam locomotives also represent a more elegant and stylish age. It is little wonder that many books and films set on trains, such as *Murder on the Orient Express*, choose a steam train for their location. Many of the most famous steam engines have been preserved for a long time after they stopped being commercially useful. They are owned by private railroad preservation companies or are looked after in transportation museums, where they are available for all to see.

The Rocket

The first successful steam train was the Rocket, built by Robert Stephenson in 1829. It established the supremacy of steam over horse-drawn trains by winning the Rainhill contest. It worked on England's Liverpool and Manchester Railroad until the end of 1830, when the Northwestern replaced it.

Classic U.S. Design

This train (*left*), designed by E. S. Norris in the 1860s, has many features that make U.S. steam trains instantly recognizable. Norris designed his trains to deal with the sharp bends and gradients of the U.S. railroad system. One strategy was to give them small wheels.

The Hiawatha

Nobody knows which steam train first reached 100 miles (160 km) per hour. In 1893, a U.S. locomotive claimed to reach a top speed of 112 miles (180 km) per hour. Eleven years later, in 1904, a train in Britain was supposed to have reached 102 miles (164 km) per hour. Neither of these claims can be verified. The first train designed to go faster than 100 miles (160 km) per hour was the Hiawatha. It began service in 1935 and ran between Chicago and Minneapolis/St. Paul. It reached an average speed of 80 miles (129 km) per hour during part of the 412-mile (663-km) journey.

The Flying Scotsman

The Flying Scotsman is probably the most famous steam train in Britain. The train was built in 1923 and ran nonstop between King's Cross station in London and Edinburgh in Scotland, which was the longest nonstop run in the world. The Flying Scotsman was eventually withdrawn in 1963, after sixty years of service. In 1988–1989, it went on a tour of Australia, where it set the record for the longest nonstop run for a steam train, a distance of 422 miles (679 km).

The Mallard

The fastest steam locomotive is the streamlined, Pacific-type train called the Mallard. It was built by British engineer Sir Nigel Gresley (1876–1941) in 1938. In the same year, while traveling between London and Edinburgh, it set a new world record for steam trains with a speed of 126 miles (203 km) per hour.

The Evening Star

The Evening Star, the last steam train to be built in Britain, went on the rails in March 1959, the year before all steam locomotives were withdrawn from Canadian railroads. Although built as a freight train, it also was used as a passenger train. In 1966, the Evening Star was withdrawn from service. Two years later, all steam trains stopped running on British railroads.

One effect that steam locomotives had on major cities was to allow people to live farther from the center of the city, where most of them worked. Many suburbs were the direct result of railroads. This expansion created its own problems, however, when city centers became congested with people and traffic. Building the first underground railroad system in London, in 1863, was an ideal solution. It ran from Paddington to Farringdon Street, a distance of nearly 4 miles (6.4 km). The success of London's underground system encouraged other cities concerned about crowded streets to build similar systems. Today, the increase in the number of automobiles has created new environmental concerns, and many cities are putting more money into their underground railroad systems.

Smoky Tunnels

This picture (*right*) from 1863 shows a steam train running on the London **underground**. The tunnel appears clean, but steam trains in enclosed spaces could be very unpleasant. A mechanism that diverted smoke into the water tank partly solved the problem. By the end of the nineteenth century, using electric trains on underground systems meant journeys became much cleaner.

Cut and Cover

This picture (*left*) from 1868 shows how the British constructed the underground railroad in London. They used a system called cut and cover. They dug a hole, built the tunnel arches, and covered the hole over again.

U.S. Subways

This picture (*right*) shows people entering a **subway** in New York City. With more than 240 miles (386 km) of track, the New York subway is certainly the largest underground system in the United States, but it was not the first to be constructed in the United States. The first U.S. subway was built in Boston in 1897. New York City opened its first subway in 1904.

The Paris Metro

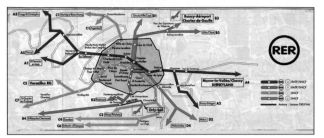

The underground railroad in Paris, called the **Metro**, opened in 1900. Stations in the center of Paris are very close together. Using glass and cast iron, famous architect Hector Guimard (1867–1942) designed the distinctive Metro station entrances in the art nouveau style.

Squashed in Tokyo

The subway system in Tokyo opened in 1927. It is, perhaps, best known for trains so crowded that people are employed to push passengers into the cars to make sure that as many people as possible squeeze in.

The Moscow Metro

The Moscow Metro is one of the most lavish underground systems in the world, but it had its price. It was built in the early 1930s at the order of Soviet leader Joseph Stalin. Many of the laborers who built the Moscow Metro were prisoners. The work was hard, and thousands died during construction.

Confusing Maps

The first maps of the London underground were difficult to understand. In the 1930s, London engineer Harry Beck (1903–1974) created a new map. The stations were linked by straight lines, and the tracks were much larger than if drawn to scale.

After the 1950s, railroads quickly became a **relic** of a declining industrial past. Automobiles gave people a far more flexible form of transportation. Airlines offered both higher levels of comfort and lower prices to compete with long-distance passenger trains. In Britain, railroad tracks have been cut by half, from 20,000 miles (32,180 km) in 1950 to about 10,000 miles (16,090 km) in 1990. The United States has reduced its tracks from 224,300 miles (360,975 km) to 162,700 miles (261,840 km). In the past few years, however, trains have begun to fight back. Trains are faster and more reliable than ever, and environmental concerns have made many governments reconsider the value of railroads.

Above It All

One way trains reduce congestion in cities is by using overhead **monorails**. Monorail trains have been running for many years. The first one was built in Germany in 1901 and is still used today. Some modern monorails run by collecting electricity from the sides of the rails. Others are **Maglev trains** with magnetic power lines.

The Railplane

In the 1920s, George Bennie (1892–1957) built an experimental train near Glasgow, Scotland. The wheels ran along a monorail suspended above the train. A propeller at the back pushed the train forward. Although the experiment was a success, the train was abandoned because it was too expensive to develop.

Gas Turbine Trains

Gas **turbine** trains work by mixing gas with air and igniting it. The air expands, escapes, and spins a rotor that provides the engine with power. The first gas turbine train was built in 1941 in Switzerland, but it was abandoned because it was too expensive to run.

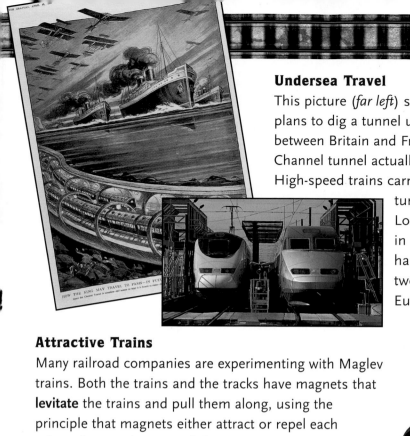

Undersea Travel

This picture (*far left*) shows that there have been plans to dig a tunnel under the English Channel between Britain and France for many years. The Channel tunnel actually was completed in 1992. High-speed trains carry passengers through the tunnel, from the center of London to the center of Paris, in about three hours. The right-hand picture (*left*) shows the two high-speed trains, the Eurostar and TGV.

Attractive Trains

Many railroad companies are experimenting with Maglev trains. Both the trains and the tracks have magnets that **levitate** the trains and pull them along, using the principle that magnets either attract or repel each other. This Maglev train (*below*) is on the Yamanashi Maglev test line in Japan, which opened in 1996. The line is more than 26 miles (42 km) long. The trains can travel nearly 350 miles (563 km) per hour.

Traveling at High Speeds

Many high-speed trains require expensive new tracks. In Italy, a high-speed train called the Pendolino (*right*) was developed with a special tilting mechanism to deal with bends in the rails. It runs on two lines, one between Turin and Venice and the other between Milan and Naples. It has a maximum speed of 185 miles (298 km) per hour.

Who was the first person to die in a railroad accident?

The Liverpool and Manchester Railroad opened on September 15, 1830. Eight trains stood ready to pull more than six hundred invited guests, including the British Prime Minister and the Duke of Wellington. Another guest was William Huskisson (1770–1830), the member of Parliament for Liverpool and an influential backer of the railroad. He stepped out into the path of one of the trains and became the first person to be killed by a train.

Which countries have the smallest railroad systems?

Several countries in the world have no railroad system at all, including Bhutan and Rwanda. Some countries have tiny railroad systems. The principality of Monaco has only 1 mile (1.6 km) of track. Even though railroads in the United States have been declining over the past few decades, the United States still has the most track of any country in the world. In 1990, U.S. railroad companies had more than 162,000 miles (260,700 km) of track.

Where is the straightest piece of railroad track?

One of the most luxurious train rides in the world is on the Indian-Pacific Line, which runs between Perth and Sydney in Australia, a journey of 2,386 miles (3,840 km). The train is more than 2,600 feet (792 m) long, and first-class passengers have their own private rooms with bathrooms and toilets. During the journey, passengers travel in a straight line for 297 miles (478 km). This is the longest piece of straight railroad track in the world.

How were headlights developed?

The United States was the first country to put headlights on the front of its trains. In the early 1830s, Horatio Allen (1802–1899), who started the South Carolina Railroad Company, placed a burning pile of pinewood in an iron basket on his trains. By the time of the Civil War in the United States, most headlights used oil for fuel and had powerful reflectors to throw the light forward.

Abandoned Railroads of the United States
www.abandonedrailroads.com
Go on an abandoned railroad hunt. Follow links to books, park trains, and more.

Railroad Museum of Pennsylvania Education Gateway
www.rrmuseumpa.org/education/
Find out about railroad careers, social issues, music, economics, and more.

Trakkies for Kids who Love Trains
www.trakkies.co.uk
Games, brain teasers, things to do for kids of all ages.

Surfing the Net with Kids: Trains
www.surfnetkids.com/trains.html
The best train sites for kids, teachers, and families.

apartheid — racial segregation

boiler — the part of a steam generator where water is converted into steam

boxcars — freight cars that look like boxes on wheels

cab — the place in the locomotive where the engineer and fireman sit

coal scuttle — a tray with a pole handle for carrying heavy loads

cowcatchers — inclined frames on the front of a railroad locomotive for pushing obstacles off the tracks

crank — the bent part of an axle or shaft or an arm set at right angles to the end of a shaft that produces the circular motion that moves the wheels of a train

cylinder — the piston chamber in an engine

diesel fuel — a heavy mineral oil used as fuel in diesel engines

driving wheels — the wheels connected to the pistons, which do the work of moving the locomotive

dynamo — a generator

engineer — a person who drives a train

firebox — the chamber in the boiler that contains the fire

fireman — the person in charge of keeping the fire going under the boiler of a steam train

flatcars — the simplest kind of railroad cars with a flat bottom and no covering

freight trains — railroad trains that carry goods

fuel injection — a system for injecting a precise amount of atomized fuel into the cylinders or the intake airstream of an internal combustion engine

gandy dancers — laborers who laid railroad tracks; named after a type of shovel they used

gauge — the distance between the rails of a railroad track

junctions — the places where trains can stop to change tracks, similar to street intersections

leading wheels — the small front wheels of a locomotive, often not connected to the source of power

levitate — to rise or float in seeming defiance of gravity

locomotive — a self-propelled vehicle that runs on rails and is used for moving railroad cars

Maglev trains — trains in which both the train and the tracks have magnets that levitate and pull the train

Metro — French and Russian word for subway

monorails — single rails serving as tracks for wheeled vehicles

navvy — the nickname for a laborer employed to dig canals or build railroads in England

nitroglycerin — a liquid that is very unstable and highly explosive

pantograph — a device, usually on top of a train, that collects electricity from a power source

piston — a sliding valve moving within a cylinder

Pullman car — a sleeping car on a train, named after George Pullman, who designed the first one

relic — a souvenir or remnant of a system

signal blades — the arms on the signal tower that tell a train engineer whether to stop, go, or turn

signal tower — a small tower with a cabin for the signal operator

steam engine — an engine driven or worked by steam

stoke — to add fuel to a fire in order to keep it going

streetcars — electric trains, usually consisting of just one car, that run on city streets

subway — an electric underground railway

tank cars — railroad cars that hold liquids

trailing wheels — the back wheels on a locomotive, which usually are not connected to the source of power

trolley — streetcar

turbine — a rotary engine driven by the pressure of water, steam, or air

underground — the British word for subway